THE
WORST PROVERBS

By John Bear

Illustrated by   Ed Powers

PRICE / STERN / SLOAN
Publishers, Inc., Los Angeles

ACKNOWLEDGEMENT

It is said that "The water knows not how many hands are on the pump handle." Similarly, some of the proverbs in this anthology have been penned by hands other than those of the author.

It is also said that "The most prolific author cannot run when his shoelaces have been knotted together." Accordingly, let tribute now be paid to the following persons, who have contributed an idea or perhaps two to this book.

After all, "A thousand thank yous cannot erase a single farewell." *Howard Gossage, Marion Seawell, Janet Livingstone, Arlis Stewart, E. E. Rehmus, Herb Caen, Jim Campbell, Larry Sloan, Roger Price, George Hart and Marina Bear.*

PROVERB: (From the Latin *proverbium* — "set of words put forth") A short, pithy saying in frequent and widespread use, expressing a well-known truth or fact. Synonyms: saying, maxim.

Once he invented language — possibly a mistake — Man has used it for two essential purposes: (a) to transmit functional information as in "Pass the salt," "What time is it?" and (b) to formulate rules of conduct (Proverbs).

Every Age of Man has had Proverbs that both reflected and molded the culture of that period.

There was the Age of Beauty (" Beauty and style and harmony depend on simplicity." — *Plato).* Then the Age of Stoicism ("Ouch, that didn't hurt!" — *Marcus Aurelius).* The Age of Reason ("I think therefore I am." — *Descartes).* The Age of Certainty ("We are not amused." — *Queen Victoria).* And so on.

Today we live, I would say, in the Age of Unreason, or perhaps the Age of Confusion, which began with Howard Cosell and the discovery of Ring Around the Collar. We desperately need some appropriate proverbs to see us through this puzzling period.

This small volume fulfills that need. With a vengeance. Memorize it. It couldn't hurt.

Roger Price

The present time
is always now

Thin paper
weighs less

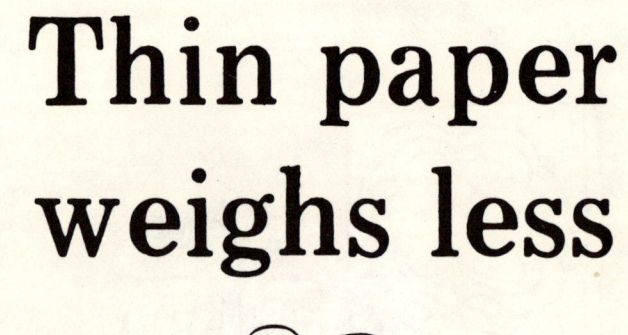

Mistakes
are often
stepping stones
to failure

Lightning never strikes

twice
at the same
time

When knowledge steps in, ignorance leaves

&

The hand that turns
the doorknob
opens the door

A surgeon does not work with boxing gloves

Even the brightest day ends in darkness

A man must have possessions
before he can disavow them

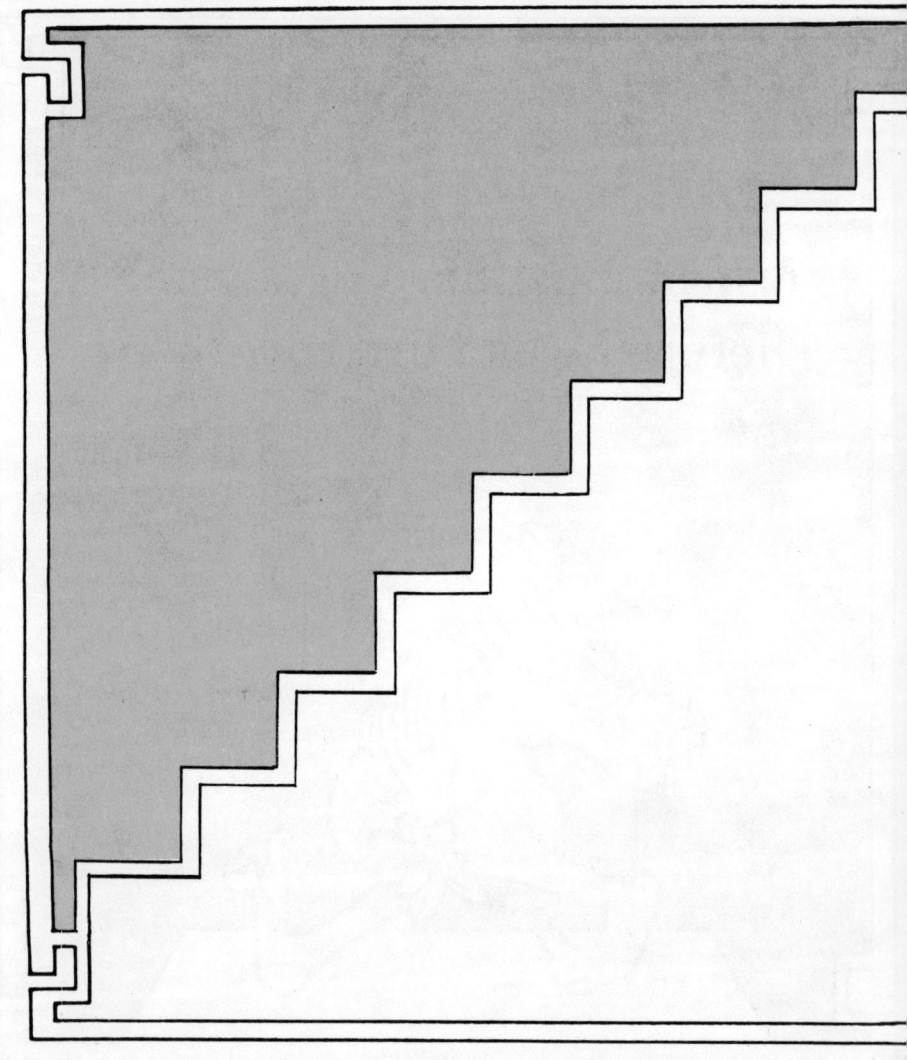

It is the

inquisitive man
who is a pest

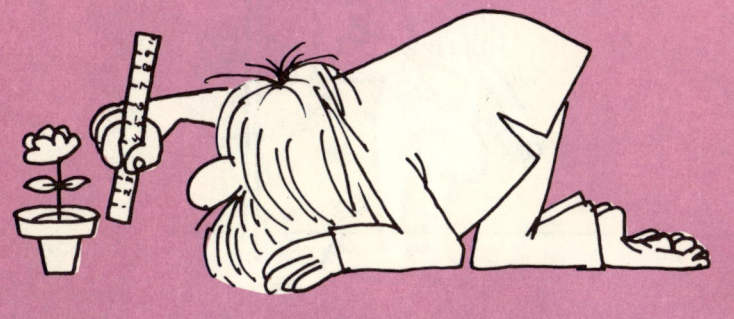

A half-full cup does not overflow

A one-armed man deals

cards slowly

The mightiest of sharks is helpless in the desert

He who depends
upon no other
may truly
be called self-reliant

He is best secure from dangers who is well-guarded

Many pages
make
a thick book

～

He who desires to
does not wish to

become rich
remain poor

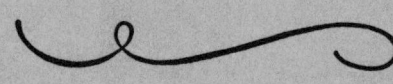

An empty cask is a good place to put old magazines

He who labors long gets a slipped disc

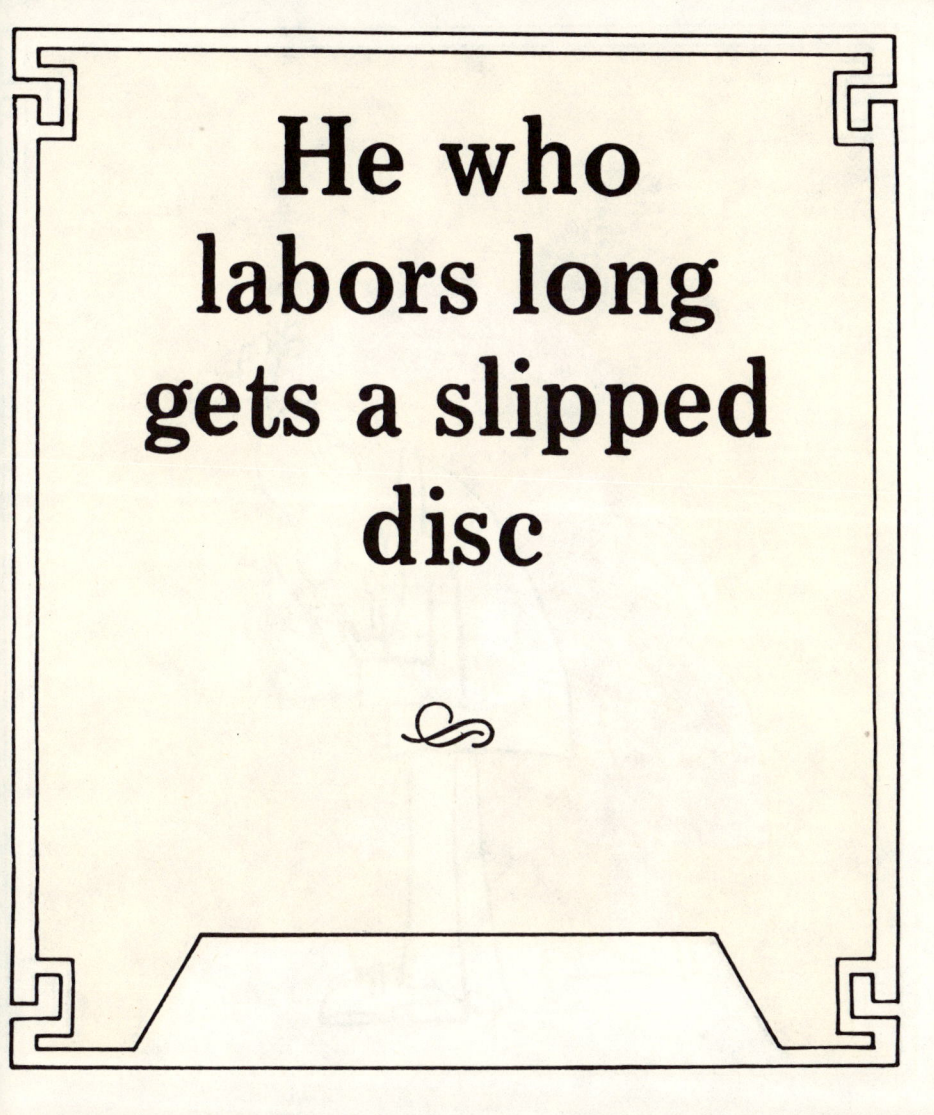

A fly does not land
in a boiling pot

The harp is gold, the clarinet black

**Even the oldest
man who ever
lived, died**

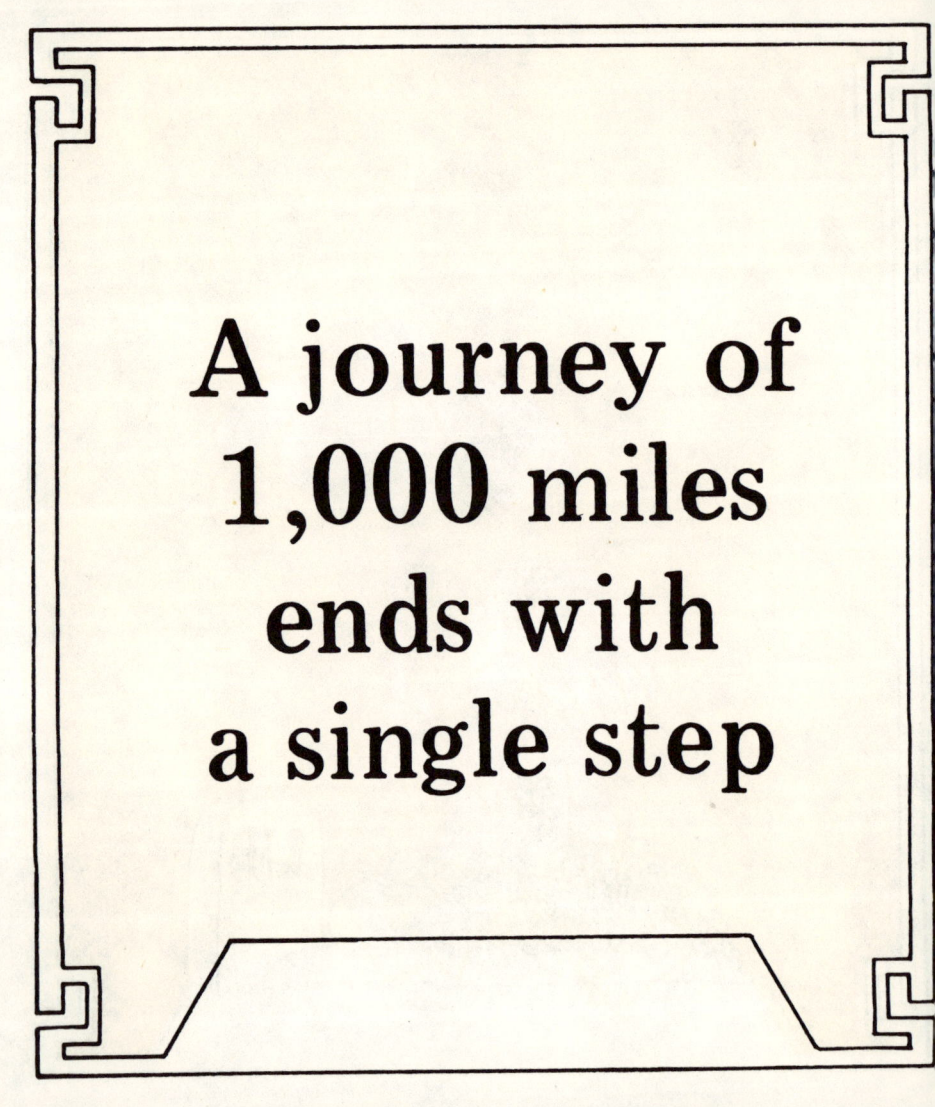

A journey of
1,000 miles
ends with
a single step

This book is published by:

PRICE / STERN / SLOAN
Publishers, Inc., Los Angeles

whose other splendid literary classics include:

**THE WORLD'S WORST JOKES
THE WORLD'S WORST GOLF JOKES
THE WORLD'S WORST KNOCK KNOCK JOKES
THE WORLD'S WORST DOCTOR JOKES
THE WORLD'S WORST PSYCHIATRIST JOKES
THE WORLD'S WORST ELEPHANT JOKES
THE WORLD'S WORST MONSTER JOKES
THE WORLD'S WORST MORON JOKES**

They are available wherever books are sold, or may be
purchased directly from the publisher by sending $1.25,
plus 50 cents for handling and mailing, to:

PRICE / STERN / SLOAN
Publishers, Inc.

**410 North La Cienega Boulevard
Los Angeles, California 90048**